Fairy
Tid-bits

By: Elizabeth Saenz

ISBN-13: 978-1482651713

THIS BOOK IS FOR

Lucas, Alexandria, and Victoria

May you always experience bits of magic
in your life.

CONTENTS

MY DEEP GRATITUDE

This book would not be possible without the help, love, and support of :

Ryan Saenz, The Bavermans, Darshan Baverman, Verónica Rosado Miñarro, Florence Sibley, Elizabeth Anne Hartman, Carolyn Woods (who asked for Fairy Tid-bits in the first place), Leslie Woods (for her mushroom story), the many friends and followers online, and of course The Fairies

Welcome into the magical world of Fairy. I have been seeing, talking to, playing with, and learning from the Fairies my whole life. I came to realize that most people did not know a lot about Fairies. There were many things I took for granted as basic knowledge that I assumed everyone had. So I posted Fairy Tid-bits on my Facebook page. These were little bits of knowledge, factoids, or information I had gathered over the years. After a year of doing these many people asked if I would publish a collection of the Fairy Tid-bits that they could keep and use as a reference. That is how this book came into form. I have organized them into four categories. **Fairy Basics** has bits of information about Fairies in general. These often have come from questions that people have asked the Fairies about themselves. **The Many Names of Fairy** has bits of myths from around the world. Fairies can be found in every culture and this is just a skim off the top of what you can find. **The Natural World** has bits of factoids about elementals and the energy of the elements as they relate to Fairy. The last section is **Interacting With The Fairies**. Here is where you will find bits that will help you interact with the Fairies around you. You will also find two meditations that can help you open and connect to the Fairies. You can read this book from start to finish or jump around out of order. After all this book is about the Fairies and they are not much for following order. The important thing is to have fun.

FAIRY

BASICS

Fairy Tid-bit
#1

Often when you hear Fairy the image of a pixie or an elegant Tuatha DeDannan is what a person pictures. There are so many other beings that are a part of the Fairy Realm and I use the term Fairy to label them. In fact every culture has "wee people" or giants in mountains or nature spirits that are a part of the Fairy Realm. Djinns (Genies), Brownies, Trolls, Goblins, Elves, Sodows, MinaHuna, Mermaids, Leprechauns, and more are all available to connect with in the Fairy Realm.

Fairy Tid-bit
#2

Some Fairies love animals while others are not as connected to them. Some Fairies adore plants while others have no interest. Some Fairies long to connect with Humanity while others have different focuses to tend too. Be aware that the Fairies connecting with you are choosing to connect with you in the way that best resonates with them.

Fairy Tid-bit #3

The Fairies do love the Earth and support environmentalism. However this is not their only focus and they are not judgmental of humanity for it. They have said many times over "Nature always wins". If Humans continue to pollute and use up our resources then we will be destroyed and the Earth will regain balance. Humanity has been shifting into better practices and they acknowledge this too. They also believe that all damage done is reversible and will be reversed by the many beings working for the betterment of the planet.

Fairy Tid-bit #4

Fairies can have many types of wings. I have seen ones that resemble wings you would find on a bee, dragonfly, butterfly, fly, bat, dragon, bird and just about any other type of animal. They can be more like flipper or fins. I've seen tentacles. The wings may resemble something from nature like leaves, twigs, vines, or flowers. They could be just energetic and look like a hologram. Then there are some fairies that don't have wings at all.

Fairy Tid-bit #5

The idea of Fairy blood is true. The Fairies say that they have crossed over and fell in love with humans. They have taken a human form and bred into human bloodlines. I have also been told that certain blood lines have Fairy energy mixed in them because of a bond that they share with Fairy. Over generations fairy energy has been encoded in their DNA.

Fairy Tid-bit
#6

Fairies are not beyond the emotions we experience. They feel them strongly but know how to let them pass and not be ruled by them. They do love strongly and deeply and help us do the same.

Fairy Tid-bit
#7

Fairies do not die the way you and I and plants and animals do. Most of them do not have a physical form to get sick or break or decay. Even the ones with a physical form are not taking the same physical form as us. Of course they would say our ideas of physical form, death, and reality in general are really illusions but that is a longer topic.

Fairy Tid-bit
#8

Fairies seem beautiful or exotic. Sometimes we perceive them as horrid and frightening. Fairies just are. Like with most people it is our judgments and limitations that get projected out on to them. In the land of Fairy it is important to keep an open mind.

Fairy Tid-bit
#9

Fairies are seen as tricksters who can not be trusted. I don't believe this to be true; at least not the whole truth. The information we have now about these beings has been passed down, usually verbally, for many generations with new stories being woven in. Often you are dealing with a combination of the perspective of the person who is telling the story mixed with the person hearing it. When you add in the different societal beliefs and the different religious beliefs then you get an interesting interpretation.

Fairy Tid-bit
#10

Do Fairies ever get sick? Their answer to me was "not in the way Humans do". They do have adverse reactions to certain energies but it does not affect their form just their emotions.

Fairy Tid-bit
#11

Fairies like statues and pictures of themselves. Think about how humans love to view different artists' renditions of the human form. They feel the same about the fairy form.

Fairy Tid-bit #12

Fairies get the reputation for being not deep or just being fluff. I believe this comes form the fact that they find joy in what they do and enjoy being silly and playful. Why we Humans have decided this is not important or not serious to our survival, I'm not sure. From what I can tell it is one of the most important lessons for us to learn.

Fairy Tid-bit
#13

The Fairies can use nature; animals, trees, flowers, etc, as a way to communicate with Humans. If you feel drawn to some part of nature be still and see what it is telling you.

Fairy Tid-bit #14

The Fairies remind me often the time and space as we perceive it is really a Human concept. They sort of understand how it works and can operate in it if they must but it is not their true perspective of things. I think this is why there are so many stories of humans being lost in Fairy. They only tell me that their experience is more fluid with less structure.

Fairy Tid-bit
#15

Fairy wings are the manifestation of the Divine flow of energy to and from the Fairy. They can help express the energy of the Fairy. A tree Fairy may have leaf wings, or twigs, or pieces of fruit. Leaf wings could represent the energy of growth. Twig wings can be the energy of core strength or reaching out for help. Fruit wings could bring forth the energy of sweetness or nurturing. These are just examples and can differ from Fairy to Fairy.

Fairy Tid-bit
#16

Fairies are often seen dancing, appear at dances, and invite humans to join dances. What is this connection between Fairies and dance? It has something to do with being free to express yourself without words. A place where you let your shyness or fear melt away and what is in your soul pour out. Join the dance.

Fairy Tid-bit #17

The easiest Fairies to connect to are the ones that are most connected to your energy already. These might be the Fairies that occupy the area you live, or the Fairies from where you were born, or the Fairies that your bloodlines are from. The geography of an area holds certain energy and attracts certain Fairies and Humans.

Fairy Tid-bit
#18

Dragons are not part of the Fairy Realm but are one of a few beings that can spend time there. They enjoy the energy of the Realm and spending time with the Fairies. This is why artists are often inspired to draw the two together.

Fairy Tid-bit
#19

Fairies love Humanity and believe in us and our natural Divinity. They know we (us and them) are all evolving together. It is through the understanding of ourselves as individuals and the acceptance of each other that we grasp the concept of the One.

Fairy Tid-bit
#20

Puck, imps, the tricksters, the fools, all of these get called "devilish". They are often seen as un-trust worthy. I see these beings as the ones that break us free from our limited thinking. A fresh perspective comes from playing the Fool to a prankster Fairy. I find this often to be a most cherished gift.

Fairy Tid-bit
#21

Fairies spark magic and wonder in Humans. Just the idea or the picture of a Fairy can bring joy and magic to the mind and heart of Humans. Never under estimate the power this has.

Fairy Tid-bit
#22

We humans like to separate and classify the
energies. These are Fairies, these are Angels,
these are Aliens. There is much more
blending that happens and we are all the
Divine. We are all a piece of the same puzzle.

Fairy Tid-bit #23

When I discuss light and dark I do not mean positive and negative or good and bad. Light and dark is a way of describing the two sides. The light are the ones in the light that you see the most often and are the most obvious. The dark are the ones you dig for or are triggered when they are needed. Fairies have light and dark sides as do humans. Humanity are the only ones who have judgments about them.

Fairy Tid-bit
#24

The Fairies often ask us to step out of our labels and judgments and look at things differently. Sometimes you need to fly high to see the bigger picture. Sometimes you need to lay on your back and look up for a new perspective. When you free yourself from your self made restrictions it is easier for them to help you.

Fairy Tid-bit
#25

You cannot expect Fairies to react like humans do. They have a different reality and perspective. Likewise don't expect all humans to react as you do, they too have a different reality and perspective.

Fairy Tid-bit
#26

Instead of looking for what you think a Fairy should look like, open to what Fairies are around you now. State that you are willing and welcome them. Those that want to work with you will appear. The full moon is a perfect time for this but do it when it feels right to you.

Fairy Tid-bit
#27

When you open to new possibilities of what a fairy can look like, or how you can communicate, you create new opportunities to connect that you were closed to before.

Fairy Tid-bit
#28

Each Fairy is very different from the next. They do have one thing in common; a love of all nature which includes humanity. How they each express this will be very different.

Fairy Tid-bit
#29

Fairies have said they don't tend to label things too often including names for themselves. It seems that some have names and some say "you can call me" as to indicate this is a name for their relationship with the Human. I think of it in the way that close friends and family will often give nicknames to people.

Fairy Tid-bit
#30

I don't believe fairies are in conflict with any religion. It is like saying trees are in conflict with religion. Fairies just are a natural energy that exists.

Fairy Tid-bit
#31

Fairies are not here to trick, test, or manipulate you. They interact with humanity to shift our perspective, help us evolve, and create more magic in the world. It is important to look at the challenges of life and know there are solutions; you just have to expand your mind to find it.

Fairy Tid-bit
#32

The Fairy Realm can seem scary and topsy turvy! This is because magic is not always rational and passion does not follow a straight line.

Fairy Tid-bit
#33

Different Fairies can be active at different times of day and night. It might be time to switch up when you connect with The Fairies if you always connect at the same time. Of course it could be that these are the Fairies you are supposed to connect with. You can decide.

Elizabeth Saenz

Fairy Tid-bit
#34

There are as many male fairies as there are
female even though they are often portrayed
in art as female. I believe this is because the
Fairy invokes energies that are often related
to the feminine; intuition, magic, sensuality,
and creative juices.

Fairy Tid-bit #35

Fairie, Faerie, Faery, Fairy, Fae, or little people. No matter how you spell it or label them, they are just as magical.

Fairy Tid-bit
#36

Do Fairies keep pets? The answer I received when I asked this question was that they had companions similar to a relationship we have with our pets. Often there is a energetic connection that leads other beings to work with them in this dynamic.

Fairy Tid-bit
#37

Every day you are alive can be a celebration.
The Fairies celebrate each magical moment
and ask us to join in the dance. Worry and
stress are Human concepts that they do not
experience.

Elizabeth Saenz

THE MANY NAMES OF FAIRY

Fairy Tid-bit #38

In Haitian Voudu (known as Voodoo to some) are a family of beings called the Guedes. I consider these beings as part of the Fairy Realm. The most interesting is Mama Brigitte who is almost identical to the Celtic Tuatha De Dannan Brigit. I think this illustrates how different cultures canconnect with a certain energy and interpret it differently.

Fairy Tid-bit
#39

As long as we have had modern technology there have been stories about beings who have messed with it. Think about the gremlins of WW2 or even that Twilight Episode with the plane and Captain Kirk. I have spoken with a few beings I would call techno Fairies. We have to remember that our computers contain crystals; that everything we think of as man-made and maybe not natural still has a natural base. The Fairies have used my computer, the radio, my MP3 player, TV, and video games to communicate with me or get my attention. They see the benefit of these tools as ways of communication.

Fairy Tid-bit #40

The Tuatha De Dannan was a race of beings that lived on Earth. Some believe they were a more advanced human, some think they were something else. The Celtic belief is that, instead of warring with the civilization that was coming into their territory, they just moved into the otherworld with the Fairy. The Tuatha De Dannan are the Gods and Goddesses of the Celtic people and are believed to have interacted with them to help with the evolution of our species.

Fairy Tid-bit
#41

Pixies do exist in fairy. They do not all look like Tinkerbell. Often they appear to me more "creature" like then human like. Again I say that they can appear in many forms and open to see how they wish to reveal themselves to you. I have a pixie friend that looks like a human/bee Queen. She is very elegant and very exotic to me.

Fairy Tid-bit
#42

Cupid is the energy of love in humanity and the many expressions and relationships of love. Since this is such a big energy it has been personified in both the Angelic and Fairy Realm.

Fairy Tid-bit #43

I think many beings who are referred to as Giants are actually Fairy. These beings are often said to live within or as mountains. They are said to guard certain natural places. They can be seen as ugly but are often used to frighten and protect certain parts of the world. In almost every case I have heard Giants are demanding respect for themselves and for nature.

Fairy Tid-bit
#44

Trolls are part of the Fairy Realm. They are guardians of passage ways. Though they are often portrayed as harsh, disgusting creatures who eat rocks and goats. Though they are more intense then some other fairy beings I have also had some pleasant experiences with trolls. It is often how you approach them. As with most fairies, if you have clear good intentions in your heart then they are more open to assisting you.

Fairy Tid-bit
#45

The Apus, of Peru, are spirits that live in the mountains. They are sometimes associated with ancestors spirits and sometimes not. They have Incan origins but I am not sure they are limited to that connection.

Fairy Tid-bit #46

The Ohdows, Gahonga, and Gandayah are nature spirits that live in North America, Their stories were told by Native Americans. They were in charge of keeping spirits that lived within the Earth under control. They lived within mountains, streams, and trees.

Fairy Tid-bit
#47

The Abatwas are the Fairy of South Africa.
They resemble Humans, mainly the tribes of
the area, but are tiny. They are known to ride
on the backs of insects.

Fairy Tid-bit
#48

The Sirens are a part of the Fairy Realm.
Again the energy of who they are has been
misunderstood and twisted over the years.
They have said that their song awakens what
is in your heart. If your heart is full of fear and
anger then you will experience that. If it is lust
then that. If it is full of truth and love then that
is the gift you receive. They cannot control
how you experience it; they just sing.

Fairy Tid-bit
#49

The Menehune (or Minahuna, spelling can be tricky with Fairies) are part of the Fairy Realm. They are the nature spirits of the Hawaiian islands. They range from volcano beings to delicate flower beings. They live within the Earth and the ocean. There are many different types.

Fairy Tid-bit #50

Most of the Japanese beings I find in Fairy are that of shape shifting animals, like the Kitsune. The Kitsune is a woman who is also a fox. Often in fairytales she still has her multiple fox tails (usually nine) even when she is in human form. Kitsune are connected with the fire element and are known for gifting those that are kind to them.

Fairy Tid-bit
#51

In Russia there is a spirit of the forest called Leshii (he is similar to Pan) and is considered the protector of trees and animals. There are also Domovoi that are house sprites that help keep the house clean and assist the residents of the house.

Fairy Tid-bit
#52

St. Patrick's Day is frowned upon by many
Pagans since it is a celebration of a Catholic's
purging (including killing) of them from Ireland.
The Fairies believed this was an attack on
their connection to Humanity and the land. So
what did they do? They reclaimed the day.
They took it for themselves. What do you think
of when decorating for this day? Shamrocks,
Leprechauns, Rainbows, and pots of gold are
the first things that come to mind. It has
become a day of play, drunken debauchery,
and opening yourself to the mystical and
improbable.

Fairy Tid-bit
#53

Leprechauns are both male and female. Some can look like the old man with the pipe, hat, and buckle shoes, but they take many other forms too. I do often see them in greens and gold but not always.

Fairy Tid-bit #54

I have always loved Australia and I have wanted to connect more with the Fairies there. Most recently I have discovered Bush Sprites. I am slowly learning about them and their unique energy. They seemed to be as varied as the Fairy realm itself. As well as the mermaids that swim around there. I have also been told that Tasmania is a magical isle and a powerful Fairy place.

Fairy Tid-bit
#55

Fairies don't always appear in the form of a
being. Sometimes they are just balls of lights,
a leaf, or a water droplet. Rainbows and
iridescent lights are often a signal of Fairies
present.

Fairy Tid-bit
#56

Cinderella's Fairy Godmother is one of the most famously well known Fairies. Though the Cinderella story seems to have been around for awhile in different versions, its most famous version was written by Charles Perrault of France. He is the one credited for adding the Fairy Godmother. I have always felt she was a French Fairy who had inspired him.

Fairy Tid-bit
#57

The legend of the Tooth Fairy goes back as far as early Norse stories and traditions. It is found in many parts of the world and seems to spread wider all the time. Talk about a busy Fairy.

Fairy Tid-bit #58

The Fossegrimen is a spirit who lives in waterfalls of Scandinavia. The Fossegrimen is a magnificent musician who plays the fiddle day and night. He will also help aspiring musicians if they present a token at a waterfall in which he dwells.

Fairy Tid-bit
#59

The Valkylries were fierce beautiful maidens that helped escort warriors from our world to Valhalla. They, like the Sidhe, are transition beings who were claimed by Fairy. They are close to the fates, having an influence on Human affairs, but also working with Humanity in service.

Fairy Tid-bit
#60

I was visited by a penguin fairy (not to be confused with the animal) that wanted me to let everyone know you can find Fairies on EVERY continent including Antarctica and they also are found in parts of the Artic circle. After all Santa Clause is an elf.

Fairy Tid-bit #61

The Alux or Aluxes are Mayan nature spirits that guarded the forest. They were known to help humans and enjoyed gifts of honey and beads. They even could choose to watch over a person, family, or farm.

Fairy Tid-bit
#62

Kappas are reptilian like beings that inhabit the rivers and waters of Japan. They are about the size of a child. Seen as pranksters, dangerous, and at times helpful, they are definitely part of the Realm of Fairy.

Fairy Tid-bit
#63

The Rusalki is another water being from Russia. They are female and seen as somewhere between a succubus and a mermaid.

Fairy Tid-bit
#64

Patupaiarehe of New Zealand have as much myth and depth as the Tuatha De Dannan of the Celts. They live in the forest and mountains of New Zealand and have been interacting with the people since they first set foot on the soil. I find it interesting that they are described as "light skinned" and having red or golden hair.

Fairy Tid-bit
#65

In China there are many stories of Fairies as young women who come down from the stars or sky.

Fairy Tid-bit
#66

Fairy Myths exist in every culture. There is truth in these tales but there are also twisted truths or lies. Often these stories were used to try and control children or groups of people through fear.

Fairy Tid-bit
#67

Trolls are often portrayed as grumpy men that live under a bridge. Their beauty is very different from ours and Humans would perceive them as ugly. They are less likely to try and trick humans or goats and eat them as they are guarding the portals to fairy or the fairies that live in our realm.

Fairy Tid-bit
#68

A Genie (Djinn) can help grant your wishes, but a wiser purpose of that relationship would be to find out what your heart desires. What are the passions that burn in you?

Fairy Tid-bit #69

The Wichtlein of Southern Germany are dwarf like beings that live in the mines. One story discusses them knocking three times to signal the death of a miner.

Fairy Tid-bit #70

When discussing Hobbits with a friend I decided that they do exist and I have seen them but I often refer to them as gnomes. There are actually three very different beings that I have labeled gnomes and maybe it is time for me to re-define a couple of them.

Fairy Tid-bit
#71

I have found that I must continually expand
my idea of what a Fairy is. The question
"What is a Fairy?" is much like the question
"Who am I ?"; I would say there is no clear
definition and it is ever evolving.

THE
NATURAL
WORLD

Fairy Tid-bit #72

Snow Fairies like to grant wishes. The snow covers the town and allows everyone to rest and feel what they desire most. They work during winter which is a time of reflection and inner work. Even if there is no snow around, open to these fairies in winter.

Fairy Tid-bit
#73

Fairies don't fly in the sense that you and I think of a plane flying. They are not confined to our space and time continuum. They are not limited to a physical form the way we have chosen to be. At times they can be more physical and have wings that flutter but still the movement that propels them forward is not aerodynamics nor wind currents. The bees have learned this and it is why they are able to fly when we think they should not be able to. Fairies have said that flying is less about having wings and more about accepting you can fly.

Fairy Tid-bit #74

The Full Moon does not draw Fairies out but allows a space where our minds open enough to see them. The full moon stirs magic in our minds and hearts that allows us to see what normally we would be blind to. Let the light and shadows play in your imagination.

Fairy Tid-bit
#75

I have encountered Fairies that were connected to a certain crystal. There are ones who work with a particular type of crystal, but also just attached to one crystal too. Sometimes when a crystal "calls to someone" it is because there is a Fairy being using it as a connection point.

Fairy Tid-bit
#76

Fairies are very connected to the Earth. This is not the only planet they are connected to. Those who have Alien guides may wish to ask them about Fairies. Don't be surprised if star fairies come to connect with you at night. Remember those stars are the suns of other planets.

Fairy Tid-bit
#77

When facing natural disasters or destruction call on the Fairies. They cannot stop it but can help protect those who need it.

Fairy Tid-bit #78

Mushrooms spring up, like magic, overnight. They embody the Earth energy without being hard. They are gentle but still tough. The Fairies love to use mushrooms as a magical tool and comfortable furniture.

Fairy Tid-bit
#79

Fairies assist the energy of the Earth and her many shifts and changes. It is not a job. It is not their only focus. It is just a part of the experience and choices.

Fairy Tid-bit
#80

Fairies are beings whom embody a natural energy. When you think about natural energies think about the many forces of nature as well as the Periodic Table of Elements.

Fairy Tid-bit
#81

The light side of the earth element is grounding, nurturing, stability, growth, and abundance. The dark side of the earth is stagnation, heaviness, stubbornness, and black and white thinking. Earth is about balance so it easy to find balance between these two sides.

Fairy Tid-bit
#82

The light side of the air element is release, going with the flow, gentle shifting, and daydreaming. The dark side of the air is burst of deep emotion, pushing over the top of others, and being so loud you cannot hear guidance. The air element is often tied to our mental states.

Fairy Tid-bit
#83

Not only do Fairies help protect nature, they
help rebuild it too.

Fairy Tid-bit
#84

The eclipse is a good time to feel the balance
of the elements as they all align with each
other. Ask the Fairies to help you see where
you may need a little balance in your own life.

Fairy Tid-bit
#85

Each star is a sun and each sun has a fairy
that works with its energy. When you look
upon the stars remember this. When you feel
the warmth of our sun remember this.

Fairy Tid-bit
#86

Animals can be a bridge for the Fairies to connect to humanity. If you feel like you are having trouble hearing, or feeling, or seeing them; ask your cat, dog, horse, or the animals in nature around you to help. You never know, they may turn out to be a Fairy in disguise.

Fairy Tid-bit
#87

Light is the combination of fire and air. It can feed a tree, make a rainbow with water, and transmit information. Light can be a great way to play with the fairies. You can catch it in crystals, burn candles, or find glittery things that sparkle in the light.

Fairy Tid-bit
#88

Fairies can see the abundance that nature provides around them and use it to the best of their ability. It is one of many things they are teaching humanity.

Fairy Tid-bit
#89

My aunt had mushrooms popping up all over her lawn. She told the Fairies that they were going to be mowed down and could they please put their mushroom houses somewhere safe. A couple days later there was a HUGE collection of mushrooms safely placed in the dirt in her planter. Communication is key with all beings. Ask and they will listen. Listen and they will speak.

Fairy Tid-bit
#90

Clouds are a great way for air Fairies to communicate with you. Look to the sky for inspiration. Clouds can create a picture, but they also can transmit information. I believe this is why, when trying to think hard, we often look up.

Fairy Tid-bit
#91

Sun fairies are very active where it is summer
in the world, but they are also present when
joy is needed. Vitamin D helps your joy and
can be made by your body from the light of
the sun. I think the sun fairies have a hand in
that.

Fairy Tid-bit #92

If you want the weather to shift you can ask the Fairies for a break in the rain, a few clouds, or a breeze when it is too hot.

Fairy Tid-bit
#93

The fairies who are connected to the energy of the rose have multiple energies they work with. They can help with love, the Divine feminine, protection, heart opening, and sharing. Just the image of a rose can help connect you.

Fairy Tid-bit
#94

On the Solstice the veil is thin between the realms. This is a great evening to leave a gift for the Fairies and thank them for their help.

Fairy Tid-bit
#95

The wisdom of a cherry blossom Fairy on how to find the balance of nature: Trust that the crows who steal the cherries from the top of the tree will still leave cherries for you to pick. There is plenty for every being and we must see the world that way.

Fairy Tid-bit
#96

Healing yourself and the land go hand in hand
AND the Fairies will help with both.

Fairy Tid-bit
#97

There are Fairy portals that open and close sporadically and then others that remain a constant. They happen in trees, ponds, and many other places, including man-made Fairy doors or houses.

Fairy Tid-bit #98

A Tree Nymph often has features of a tree but is still different then an Ent which is a tree being, but both are Fairy. If you need grounding and help with home or stability ask the tree beings and nymphs.

Fairy Tid-bit
#99

The Fairies lounge on flowers, sleep in trees, and float on the surface of the ocean. They understand that relaxing is as important as doing.

Fairy Tid-bit
#100

The magic of the Fairies is not an unnatural occurrence. In fact their magic is the very fabric of our natural world. This magic is in the miracle of every creation. It is compacted into every seed, every egg, and every stone. Inside every cell is a bit of magic waiting to be accessed.

Fairy Tid-bit
#101

Every significant shift in nature has a Fairy, or group of Fairies, who work specifically with that energy. If you are worried about a natural phenomenon or wanting to deepen your understanding of an event call on the Fairy or Fairies that work with that energy.

Fairy Tid-bit
#102

The Fairies of lightening also work with the energy of epiphanies and insight. They help with the bright flash that lights up our inner sky in our darkest moments.

Fairy Tid-bit
#103

The honey bee is a Earthly creature that embodies much of the fairy energy. Both are known to travel betweens the realms, and both remind Humanity that anything is possible, even if you can't rationally explain it.

Fairy Tid-bit #104

The Genies (or Jinns) work with the energy of manifesting. They do help grant wishes but not quite how it has been portrayed. Their main element is fire and the qualities of fire are very present in them. Remember fire can create as much as it can destroy. Sometimes things have to be destroyed to create the new. Jinns can help with all of that. They will always create from your true desire that is burning inside you, so when asking for help, be sure you are being honest with yourself about what you want because it may not turn out like you think.

Fairy Tid-bit #105

Mermaids do exist, are part of The Fairy Realm and do help people. Their main element is (obviously) water but there are some that are more connected to air. They are amazing healers, especially with emotional trauma. There are also Mermen. They help you see the treasures that have been buried deep below the darkness. Mermaids were a part of myths in many cultures. It seems that any group of people who spent time in boats on the ocean connected with these amazing beings.

Fairy Tid-bit
#106

Mermaids are not the only water fairy beings. There are Undines, Selkies, Sirens, some I don't have names for, bubble fairies, and many more. Each element seems to connect with very different fairies. Water can be a bubble floating on the breeze or a tsunami wiping out villages. We can use it to quench our thirst or drill through metal and rock. Each element has many different qualities and there are fairies for each one.

Fairy Tid-bit
#107

The light side of the fire element is hearth, warmth, nurturing, heart centered passion, and protection. The dark side of fire is rage, intensity, destruction, and wild passion. Both sides serve a purpose and you must use both when working with this energy.

Fairy Tid-bit
#108

The light side of the water element is release, cleansing, flowing gently, and being refreshed. The dark side of the water is overwhelming emotion, feeling tossed by the rapids, and instability. Usually when you are experiencing the dark side it is to get you unstuck.

Fairy Tid-bit
#109

Water Fairies help with the energy of
emotions. If you are feeling sad or stuck in
depression ask mermaids, selkies, and other
water beings to help.

Fairy Tid-bit
#110

The Fire Fairies of the Sun can have fun with
solar flares and technology. Ask them for help
if you are experiencing the adverse effects.

Fairy Tid-bit #111

When dealing with fireworks the Fairies can help. Ask them to help calm the animals, contain the fires, and protection for all the beings (including plants) around the fireworks. Then create the magic together for a spectacular time!

Fairy Tid-bit
#112

Volcanoes, large trees, and rivers can all be homes of Fairy. Look around you to find the natural Fairy Dens by your home.

Fairy Tid-bit
#113

A Fire Sprite can feel dangerous to Humans but they are actually very important. They help spark the fires of passion, start the energy of the hearth, or light your way out of the darkness. Sometimes a small spark is all we need to set our dreams ablaze.

Fairy Tid-bit
#114

Trees and beehives are known portals to the Fairy Realm, but they are not the only ones. You can find them in many places and, as our two Realms open more to each other, the numbers seem to be growing. The best place to connect to Fairy energy is the heart of a true believer.

Fairy Tid-bit
#115

The Honeybee works closely with The Fairies. They both work with the Earth's energetic grid and help ground the energy of impossibility or improbability. What does that mean? Well we Humans have fallen deeply into our scientific mind. We also have always had a drive to rationalize. To keep balance we need things we cannot understand or rationalize away.

The Fairies and bees bring us these experiences. They remind us of magic, God; energy greater then us that we are a part of. It is one of the reasons the Fairies love honey so much. It is imbued with that energy.

Fairy Tid-bit #116

Mushrooms that grow in a circle on the ground is known as a Fairy Ring. Mushrooms can be a sign that magic has been present in the spots you find them. Instead of picking, squashing, or destroying mushrooms. Stop and see if you can feel the magic that is present.

Fairy Tid-bit
#117

Fairies that are connected to a certain plant,
like the primrose or a fern, often take on
physical characteristics of the plant. I believe
this is partly because they are embodying that
energy but partly because they can hide
amongst them easier.

INTERACTING WITH THE FAIRIES

Fairy Tid-bit #118

The same spark of Divine that ignited magic in the Fairies, ignited magic in you. The Fairies love to remind us of our magical selves.

Fairy Tid-bit
#119

Fairies enjoy all types of music. Certain songs can help draw certain ones in. It is more about how the humans are reacting to the music. If it is opening your heart and mind then they will want to connect to you. If you are uncomfortable or trying to force yourself they will not be as inclined to join.

Fairy Tid-bit #120

Fairies often talk about the truth is in the paradox. They will give guidance in riddles and speak in what feel like opposites. It is like a Zen Koan. As you sit with the information and unravel it you gain the clarity you need.

Fairy Tid-bit
#121

No matter the offering the Fairies will use it.
To them it is all just energy. They can take just
about anything and shift it to be useful.

Fairy Tid-bit #122

When we are experiencing grief, sadness, or struggle we can feel the most disconnected from Fairy. It is a time when magic can feel fake and unhelpful. Often this is when the Fairies are the closest to us. If we can give in to surrendering to the energy then they can assist as we move through all our emotions. Don't fight your pain or fight to stay in it. Allow the fairies and your tears to wash it away.

Fairy Tid-bit
#123

Fairies can hide things and maybe even "trip you up" but this is not out of childish pranking behavior. This is done to help break you out of tunnel vision. This can veer you back on to your path and give you a fresh perspective. The intent is not malice but guidance.

Fairy Tid-bit #124

Why don't some people see Fairies? We see with our mind and what it decided we can see. There is a hole in the picture our eye takes in plus so much information our brain cannot process all of it, so it does some quick editing and tells us what we see. This happens in an instant. It is part of the way we survive and don't have a brain meltdown. If you want to experience this do any optical illusion. The reason they work is they expose the workings of the mind.

Fairy Tid-bit
#125

Fairies love gifts from us. Honey, crystals, cookies, and fruit are some of their favorites. There are a few who like wine or ale. I even know one who asks for french fries. What the gift is does not matter as much as the intent behind it. Are you offering it out of gratitude or for selfish reasons? It is fine if you are asking for a favor just make sure you are honoring the Fairies in the process. I often leave these gifts out on a shell or rock in my yard. Find your own way and create your own ritual for offering gifts to the Fairies. It is not necessary though. Sometimes they would rather a nice conversation with you then gifts with no interaction. Open to your connection with them and see what feels right.

Fairy Tid-bit
#126

It is true that Fairies love nature and are a part
of it. Remember that you are a part of nature
and where ever you are you can access this
energy to connect with them. Fairies have
also grown and evolved, as we have, to
embrace are ever changing world. I have
worked with fairies who focus on techno
energy and work with computers and phones
to connect with Humans. Remember there is
water molecules and natural minerals in these
devices too. Do not think because you are in a
big city or not around plants that you cannot
connect to Fairies OR that Fairies are not
present. Look for them in unexpected places
you will be pleasantly surprised.

Fairy Tid-bit
#127

Fairies can be demanding but I find them also
to be very patient. One once told me it was
because they don't experience time like us
that waiting doesn't bother them.

Fairy Tid-bit #128

Fairies can heal humans, plants, and animals. Never be afraid to call on the Fairies for help with healing.

Fairy Tid-bit #129

Children are often associated with Fairies because they are open to the idea of magic. When someone is open to possibilities then those possibilities can happen.

Fairy Tid-bit #130

We are all experiencing our own reality. No matter if Fairies exist in your reality or not they do exist. Just like someone on the other side of the world may not exist in your reality but they still exist. There is no right or wrong in "what exists" just personal preference. So if Fairies exist in your reality but not in someone else's you can both be right; right for you.

Fairy Tid-bit
#131

The fastest way to connect to the Fairies is to get aligned with your joy. Joy can be accessed differently for each person but the feeling is the same. It is the feeling of a light open heart.

Fairy Tid-bit
#132

Fairies don't have a need to "get even". The many stories talking about Fairies' revenge are misunderstood. Often it is the person not learning the lesson that is needed and the Fairy giving them another opportunity.

Fairy Tid-bit
#133

Fairies won't always come to you as a big ball of light or magically appearing maiden. Stay open to the subtle words in the wind, the whispers of the flowers, and the splashing of the waves. They are always talking to you in many ways.

Fairy Tid-bit
#134

Fairies and romance seem to go together like peanut butter and jelly. Both are concepts that some believe to be illusions. Both are ideas that bring hope, joy, and inspiration to Humanity. Both can be experienced by those who are truly ready.

Fairy Tid-bit
#135

Sometimes when Fairies "misplace"
something for you the lesson is to change
your perspective of ownership. What does it
mean to own something? Fairies are helping
us open to the balance of nature rather then
balancing a checkbook.

Fairy Tid-bit
#136

Fairies love ceremonies, offerings, and celebrations. It is nice to make a gesture of your intent or celebrate your connection. However sometimes it is better to just stop and listen to their wisdom without a bunch of hoopla.

Fairy Tid-bit
#137

Often, I find, people just need to be reassured that Fairies are real and they can connect. The connection will happen. The more you relax into it the easier it is. You will find more opportunities to connect the more you let go of how you think the connection should happen. Say you are willing and they will contact you.

Fairy Tid-bit
#138

Listening is a key ingredient to a relationship with the Fairies. You cannot just demand or command your desires and not listen to their guidance. Take a moment to quiet your mind and open your heart. You may not hear their words but you will receive guidance.

Fairy Tid-bit
#139

Often our greatest opportunities and gifts are not the ones we ask the Fairies for, but the ones that are forced onto our path. The ones we resist will always bring us the greatest treasure.

Fairy Tid-bit
#140

The Fairies bring inspiration and motivation
when we are feeling stuck. Sometimes it helps
to not focus on what you are trying to do and
instead clean up the house, go for a walk, or
stop and meditate. Then, like magic, you will
find it.

Fairy Tid-bit
#141

When you dress up like a fairy you are
opening yourself to their energy. You are
inviting them to join you for the dance of life.

Fairy Tid-bit
#142

When you create a Fairy Garden, a Fairy Altar, or a Fairy House then you are giving the Fairies an easy relaxed space for them to connect with you. You are providing a space that they can easily connect with our realm from theirs. You are also providing a gentle place for them to come if they choose to live in our world.

Fairy Tid-bit
#143

When working with a Fairy that embodies an element it is important to study all sides of that element. This will help you understand the light and dark sides of the Fairy and yourself.

Fairy Tid-bit #144

The Fairies live in their realm and ours. Be mindful of this when you enter places that seem touched by Fairy. Behave the way you would in a friend's house. Ask permission before you take things and be polite and respectful.

Fairy Tid-bit #145

There are many signs of a Fairies being present; mushrooms, rainbows, sparkles, and decorative patterns in nature. Look for the signs and see where they are in your life.

Fairy Tid-bit #146

When you experience a magical moment allow it to grow inside of you. This will attract more magic in your life. Take the fairy sighting and water it with faith and trust and soon they will be tickling your feet and whispering in your ear.

Fairy Tid-bit
#147

Fairies are all around you, dancing, playing, working, and enjoying your world. Take the time to feel them, talk to them, and acknowledge them. Then you will begin or deepen a relationship with them.

Fairy Tid-bit
#148

Fairies can help break habits and addictions. Ask for their guidance, the answer may be a shift in your diet, more self restraint, or it may be the uncovering of emotions that need to be shifted.

Fairy Tid-bit
#149

If you find little things missing, it may be a
Fairy needed to borrow it. You can leave gifts
for them to help with their physical needs
while they are here in the Earth Realm.

Fairy Tid-bit
#150

When you ask the Fairies what you can do for them, and do it, you begin a cycle of magic that will benefit both realms.

Fairy Tid-bit
#151

After you ask the Fairies for help, be patient.
Sometimes the solution and support come
immediately and sometimes it can take
awhile. The best way to assist is to get out of
their way.

Fairy Tid-bit #152

Angels are not Fairies and Fairies are not Angels. They are similar beings in the same sense that Humans are similar to Cows. Both have their place and their purpose.

Fairy Tid-bit
#153

Sometimes Humans need to cleanse themselves energetically or physically. Not because they are toxic or tainted but because they need the release to move on to their next step. When you are in the process of cleansing ask the Fairies for assistance and wisdom. Often we need to know what and why we are releasing to receive the full benefit of what we have just experienced.

Fairy Tid-bit
#154

Fairies can be very direct at times it may seem harsh. I believe that this comes from so many years of being misunderstood. If it is important they do not want any misunderstanding. Other times it is a riddle for you to discover because the realization of an answer is part of your path. No wonder they get labeled as tricky.

Fairy Tid-bit
#155

When you ask the Fairies to help you achieve something and you let go of the "how", they can fulfill it in the most amazing ways. The trick is to stay open even after things start to take form so they can continue to form.

Fairy Tid-bit
#156

A parent who believes in Fairies helps their
children still experience their magic.

Fairy Tid-bit
#157

The Fairies can be very nurturing. When you
are in a point of surrender, and have
developed a relationship with them, you will
be showered with comfort in many forms.

Fairy Tid-bit
#158

The Fairies can help you find the food that is
best for your body in this moment. It is
important to listen to your body and find the
food that will support the health of it.

Fairy Tid-bit
#159

Fairy time operates very different then Human time. Their idea of soon may not be the same as yours. If you are working with Fairy it is a lesson of being in the moment.

Fairy Tid-bit
#160

Fairies are not about falling into delusions or illusions. They bring up the truth for us to see life in a new way. They allow our heart to speak its longing and give us clarity.

Fairy Tid-bit
#161

So often we Humans think we have to create something to experience something. The truth is we often just have to stop resisting it. The magical world is all around us. We can put up blinders or open our eyes. The Fairies don't care if we accept their existence or not.

Fairy Tid-bit
#162

Do not be like Cinderella and wait till you are falling apart to ask your Fairy Godmother for help. All you must do is surrender to help and ask for what you need. Then accept it when it appears.

Fairy Tid-bit
#163

Fairies celebrate each other for being the authentic natural selves. We should follow their lead.

Fairy Tid-bit
#164

Fairies can't and won't dissolve every challenge. They can cover it with sugar and make it easier to go down.

Fairy Tid-bit
#165

Fairy may send you messages and nudges
that don't make rational sense. When you
follow these signs you can experience
something magical.

Fairy Tid-bit
#166

The Fairies are misplacing our keys, jewelry, or important papers to get our attention. Instead of trying to push through an energy, take the moment to check in with them. These are the times we gain insight and re-align with the universal flow.

Fairy Tid-bit
#167

Time moves differently for Fairies. People who are connected with Fairies may experience weird time anomalies. If you feel like you don't have enough time or are being run by your schedule. Take a moment to stop and breathe, connect with nature in some way, and ask the Fairies to help.

Fairy Tid-bit
#168

Fairies enjoy their "work". They follow their passions and play in it and rest in it. Take a lesson from them.

Fairy Tid-bit
#169

Fairies love to assist Humans in productive experiences. Before you fix up your garden, clean your house, or sit down to create, ask if there is a Fairy who would like to assist you and open to their influence.

Fairy Tid-bit
#170

What we believe is impossible exists outside of our limited experience. Ask the Fairies to show you the possibilities and do your best to not doubt what they present to you.

Fairy Tid-bit #171

Not all Fairies have wings. Not all Fairies grant wishes. Not all Fairies are working with Humans. Keep an open mind when connecting to Fairies and remember that beauty is in the eye of the beholder.

Fairy Tid-bit
#172

There is an exception to every rule. Trust the truth that rings in your heart. Allow the Fairies to bring you your own bits of wisdom.

Heart/Wing Meditation

Sit comfortably, with your eyes closed, and take three deep breaths. Visualize a beautiful light in the center of your being, in the middle of your heart. See this light expanding out the middle of your back and becoming wings or tendrils. Allow these to create a space for wonderful God light to pour into your body. Notice this light filling up your chest, you do not have to pull or push the energy it just flows gently in. Let this energy rise up and over your shoulders, down your arms, and out your hands. Feel the energy rising up your throat and neck, into your head, and flowing out the top. Now see the energy flowing down from your chest through your stomach, down your spine, over your belly, and into your hips. See this energy streaming down your legs over your knees, down into your feet, and out your toes. See all this energy pouring out of your body and into the Earth. Watch as the energy goes deep down into the Earth and connects with its crystalline core. Allow this energy to expand out, filling up the earth all the way to the surface. See this great energy expanding out through the atmosphere flowing through our universe and out into the cosmos. Let this energy get as big and go as far as it wants. Now sit in this energy and realize you are a part of it. Feel your connection to the great one-ness of the cosmos. You can ask for information or just soak up this abundant energy. When you are ready become aware of your body in the room you are sitting in, but know you are always connected to this great energy.

~~~

Fairy Garden Meditation

Sit or lay comfortably. Focus on the light in the middle of your heart space, in the middle of your being. Soon you will experience a path before you. As you walk along this path realize you are heading to a gate or a doorway of some kind. This may be just an archway or a portal. Take a moment to really discover this gateway. Now step through it. As you step forward you realize you are entering a garden. Take the time to experience the nature all around you. As you move through the garden you come upon a place to sit. You decide to relax into this space. Very quickly you realize you are not alone. There is a Fairy guide waiting to connect with you. Greet your fairy guide. Ask any questions you have but also make sure to listen. Once you have received all the information you need allow yourself to move out of the garden, through the gateway, and back down the path to your heart center. Once in your heart center take a moment to let all that you have received permeate your being on a cellular level. Now become aware of your physical body and open your eyes.

Illustration on pages 4 & 128

"Fairies in the Clover"
"Girl with trees"

By Verónica Rosado Miñarro

~

Illustration on cover and page 44

"Bubbles"

"Fairy Queen"

By Florence Sibley

~

Illustration on page 80

"Fire Fairy"

By Darshan Baverman

ABOUT THE AUTHOR

Elizabeth Saenz is a Reiki Master/Teacher, ThetaHealing Practitioner, Ordained Minister, and Fairy Channelor. She has also written *The Expanded Gateway: Messages to Expand Your Consciousness* and created *The Fairy Wisdom Oracle Deck*. When she is not attending festivals and conferences or teaching workshops, she is enjoying her life on Whidbey Island in Washington State with her husband and three children.

Please visit her website at:
www.theexpandedgateway.com
you can also follow her on Facebook and Twitter

19323032R00106